First Facts™

Everyday Character Education

Friendliness

by Kristin Thoennes Keller

Consultant:
Madonna Murphy, PhD, Professor of Education
University of St. Francis, Joliet, Illinois
Author, *Character Education in America's Blue Ribbon Schools*

Capstone
press

Mankato, Minnesota

First Facts is published by Capstone Press,
151 Good Counsel Drive, P.O. Box 669, Mankato, Minnesota 56002.
www.capstonepress.com

Library of Congress Cataloging-in-Publication Data
Thoennes Keller, Kristin.
    Friendliness / by Kristin Thoennes Keller.
    p. cm.—(First facts. Everyday character education)
    Includes bibliographical references and index.
    ISBN 0-7368-3680-2 (hardcover)
    1. Friendship—Juvenile literature. I. Title. II. Series: First facts. Everyday character education.
BJ1533.F8T38 2005
177'.62—dc22   2004020298

Summary: Introduces friendliness through examples of everyday situations where this character
    trait can be used.

Editorial Credits
Amanda Doering, editor; Molly Nei, set designer; Kia Adams, book designer; Wanda Winch,
    photo researcher

Photo Credits
Dan Delaney Photography, cover, 1, 5, 6–7, 8, 9, 10–11, 12, 13, 19
The Denver Public Library/Western History Collection, X-32259, 17
Photo Courtesy of D. J. Sconyers, 14, 15
Photodisc/Janis Christie, 20

Table of Contents

Friendliness

Dakotah is playing at the park with some friends. He notices a boy he hasn't seen before. The boy is playing alone. Dakotah asks him if he wants to play. The boy says yes. Dakotah's friendliness makes the boy feel happy and welcome.

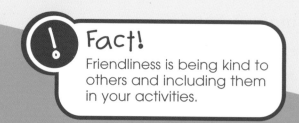

Fact!
Friendliness is being kind to others and including them in your activities.

At Your School

Being friendly helps make other people feel welcome and comfortable. Show friendliness by talking to a new student at school. **Invite** the new person to sit with you at lunch. **Introduce** him to your friends.

Fact!
Smiling is a way to be friendly without saying a word.

With Your Friends

Being friendly with your friends is usually easy. You can be friendly by sharing your things. **Compliment** your friends on things they do well.

Sometimes friends don't get
along. Friendly people don't stay
mad. Be friendly and **apologize** after
a disagreement.

At Home

Be friendly with your family. Ask your parents about their day. Share your toys with your brothers and sisters.

You can be friendly when your parents have guests. Talk with the adult guests. Play nicely with their children.

In Your Community

You and your parents can be friendly
to new neighbors. Introduce yourself
and make your neighbors feel welcome.

Friendly people make others feel good. Smile at people. Say hello. Hold doors open for people. Offer to help someone who needs it.

D. J. Sconyers

At age 12, D. J. Sconyers created a friendship project. In his project, U.S. kids sent letters and packages to kids in Lithuania, a small country near Russia.

The kids in Lithuania wrote back.
D. J.'s project helped kids in different
countries become friends.

Chief Washakie

Chief Washakie was a Shoshone Indian. He was born in the early 1800s. Chief Washakie was friendly to American settlers. He helped the U.S. government. His friendliness helped the Shoshone. The U.S. government built schools, churches, and hospitals for his tribe.

What Would You Do?

Dakotah's parents invite another family to dinner. The family has a daughter who is much younger than Dakotah. She asks him to play dolls with her. He doesn't want to play dolls. What is the friendly thing for Dakotah to do?

Fact!
International Friendship Day is the first Sunday in August.

Amazing but True!

Some people think flowers have meaning. One thousand years ago, a yellow rose stood for friendship to the Toltec people in Mexico. Today, people still give yellow roses as a sign of friendship.

Hands On: Make a Friend Book

Friends think of each other. Make a friend book and have all your friends' information in one place.

What You Need

paper
pen or pencil
notebook or computer

What You Do

1. On a piece of paper, make a list of your friends. You may also include your family on the list.
2. In a notebook or on the computer, write or type a friend's name at the top of each page.
3. On his or her page, list things you know about that friend. Include his or her address, phone number, and e-mail address. Also include that friend's birthday, hobbies, favorite color, favorite animal, and foods he or she likes.
4. List anything else you know about that friend.
5. On a friend's birthday, look up his or her address in your friend book. Send your friend a card. If you buy a present, use the list to pick out a present your friend would like.

Glossary

apologize (uh-POL-uh-jize)—to say you are sorry

compliment (KOM-pluh-ment)—to tell someone that he or she has done something well

introduce (in-truh-DOOSS)—to tell someone your name or the name of someone a person is meeting for the first time

invite (in-VITE)—to ask someone to do something or go somewhere

Read More

Nettleton, Pamela Hill. *Want to Play?: Kids Talk about Friendliness.* Kids Talk. Minneapolis: Picture Window Books, 2005.

Seder, Isaac. *Friendship.* Character Education. Chicago: Raintree, 2004.

Internet Sites

FactHound offers a safe, fun way to find Internet sites related to this book. All of the sites on FactHound have been researched by our staff.

Here's how:

1. Visit www.facthound.com
2. Type in this special code **0736836802** for age-appropriate sites. Or enter a search word related to this book for a more general search.
3. Click on the **Fetch It** button.

FactHound will fetch the best sites for you!

Index